Beloved
Heroes of the Faith

Adam and Rachel Francisco

SAINT LOUIS

Edited by Thomas Doyle and Edward Engelbrecht

This publication is available in braille and in large print for the visually impaired. Write to the Library for the Blind, 1333 S. Kirkwood Road, St. Louis, MO 63122-7295; or call 1-800-433-3954.

1 2 3 4 5 6 7 8 9 10   10 09 08 07 06 05 04 03 02 01

Contents

Introduction

In our era of great challenge, the Heroes of the Faith series highlights men and women in the Bible who overcame extraordinary difficulties. Their stories show that God chooses ordinary people—people like you—to do His extraordinary work.

The authors have taken special care not to elevate these Bible characters inappropriately. God's the true hero of each Bible story! Each session focuses on God's mercy in people's lives, especially the mercy shown through Jesus Christ.

These lessons will introduce you to the cultural setting and life story of biblical characters, examine the joys and challenges they faced, and show how God forgave, sustained, and empowered them to serve Him. Concluding activities will lead you in reviewing God's blessings in your own life.

To prepare for "Adam and Eve," read Genesis 1:27–3:24.

Worldly Powers	Dates	Bible Heroes
Satan	Creation	*Adam & Eve*
Neo-Sumerian	2000 B.C.	Abraham
Egypt, New Kingdom	1500 B.C.	Moses
Philistine Invasion	1000 B.C.	King David
Old Testament Ends	430 B.C.	
Romans	A.D. 27	Jesus Christ ✝

Cultural Setting

As the old woman tugged at the burr, a tear formed in her eye. The child's hair was so beautiful, a rich brown that shimmered like the ripples on the great Euphrates river. But a mass of gray burrs had clawed at the girl's hair as she skipped along the path to the fields that morning. They clung to the girl as if they'd never let go.

"Ouch! That hurts," the child complained.

"Yes, dear," the old woman replied.

The burr tore loose, but the child's words lodged in her heart. As she crumpled the burr between her callous fingers, she wept for the children, the grandchildren, and the great-grandchildren who had left her and spread in every direction. "They have spread," she thought. "Like the seeds of the burrs, they have spread. They grow in clusters . . . some now build walls against one another."

"Tell me a story," the little girl interrupted, hoping to delay the return to the fields. "Tell me about the trees and the fruit, and how easy it was to pick."

Meet a Hero

"God had provided Adam and me everything we needed for life. Then that wily serpent convinced me that we could and should have more. When you have everything, how could you want more? But the serpent's words were certainly convincing! To have the knowledge of good and evil would make us like God.

"God had warned us about eating from the tree of the knowledge of good and evil. But what was God trying to hide from us? Now I know what God wanted to keep from us! Evil. But we ate the fruit, and then, realizing the wrong we had done, we tried to hide from our Creator. What a joke! We were hiding from God, the One who gave us life, who knew our every movement, who preserved our lives. God found us. Knowing that we were naked, we attempted to cover our bodies. We knew evil . . . we knew shame!

"Our just God pronounced His judgment on us. We deserved His wrath. But then in His mercy God made us an incredible promise. Out of His continued love for us, those who had turned away from Him, He would provide an escape from eternal damnation. He would provide us a Savior from our sin!

8

"Whenever I think about His love, I marvel! We who had disobeyed Him continued to receive His love and mercy. We who had sinned against Him would still receive eternal life. Not because of anything we had done . . . I mean all we did was mess things up . . . but because of His enormous love for the people He had created. What wondrous love is this!"

A Promise for All

My husband and I had the privilege of "dissecting" well-known Bible passages and stories with second-language Japanese learners. We explored these stories in a new light with our Bible study leaders, Tom and Debi Going, in a new light. They showed us how Japanese characters painted beautiful pictures from the simple words or phrases of the text.

One of these characters depicted a strong image of Adam's role as husband and protector. The beautiful representation spoke volumes about Jesus—whom the Bible calls "the Second Adam"—and His willingness to protect His lambs. God's promise to send His Son for Adam has been fulfilled, and it is a promise we can cling to. How does this fact give you hope as you live out your life?

Perfect Marriage

Read Genesis 2:15–25.

1. For some people marriage and happiness seem like contradictions, but Genesis holds a different view. Why did God form Eve? How did Adam react after God brought him Eve? What does Genesis 2:24 say about a man's relationship with his wife? What do you think Adam and Eve's relationship was like prior to their fall into sin?

2. Read Genesis 3:1–7. According to God, what would happen to anyone who ate from the tree in the middle of the garden? What did the serpent say would happen if Eve ate of the fruit from the tree in the middle of the garden? What happened after Eve ate of the fruit? Why did Eve choose to eat from the tree?

3. Read Genesis 3:8–13. Adam responded to God's question concerning his hiding. What does God ask Adam next? Did Adam answer the question in its literal sense? Explain. Whom does Adam ultimately blame for his sin?

4. Read Genesis 3:14–20. After Adam and Eve disobeyed the Lord, what curses followed? In spite of their unfaithfulness, how does the Lord provide for Adam and Eve? What promise does God make to Adam and Eve?

Our Inheritance

5. From whom did you inherit your sinful thoughts, words, and actions? What are the effects of this burdensome inheritance?

6. Have you ever blamed someone or something else for your sin? How does Adam exemplify this idea that God is to be blamed for sin? From where does Scripture say sin comes?

7. What does God say to the serpent in Genesis 3:15? What does this mean? (See Galatians 4:4.) How does this threat spoken to the serpent also hold promise for you?

8. Read Genesis 3:21–24. Adam and Eve were thrown out of the garden, yet God still provided for them. How does God continue to pro-

vide for you in temporal matters? eternal matters? (See Romans 5: 14–15.)

For This Week

- Think of a promise you have made and not kept. Ask for forgiveness from the person to whom you made the promise.
- Tell your friends and family about the promise that was fulfilled through Jesus Christ.

Closing Worship

Sing stanzas 1, 3, and 5 of "Jesus Sinners Will Receive" (*LW* 229).

Jesus sinners will receive;
May they all this saying ponder
Who in sin's delusions live
And from God and heaven wander!
Here is hope for all who grieve:
Jesus sinners will receive.

When their sheep have lost their way,
Faithful shepherds go to seek them;
Jesus watches all who stray,
Faithfully to find and take them
In His arms that they may live—
Jesus sinners will receive.

Jesus sinners will receive.
Even me He has forgiven;
And when I this earth must leave,
I shall find an open heaven.
Dying, still to Him I cleave—
Jesus sinners will receive.

To prepare for "Abraham and Sarah," read Genesis 17:1–18:15; 20:1–21:12.

Worldly Powers	Dates	Bible Heroes
Satan	Creation	Adam & Eve
Neo-Sumerian	2000 B.C.	*Abraham & Sarah*
Egypt, New Kingdom	1500 B.C.	Moses
Philistine Invasion	1000 B.C.	King David
Old Testament Ends	430 B.C.	
Romans	A.D. 27	Jesus Christ †

Cultural Setting

Years had passed since she visited the well. She had grown to hate the idle conversation of the other women who gathered there twice each day. These days, she handed her tall ceramic water jug to a servant girl and sulked in her tent.

She wished she could send a daughter to the well. But she had no daughter, much less a son. That's why she hated to visit the well; she hated the banter and gossip of the other women, whose light robes encircled their matronly bodies. They had not ridiculed her—not directly. But all they could talk about was their own children or a neighbor's children. When her name came up, a great silence surrounded the well. She would dip her water hastily, hoist the jug to the top of her head, and hurry away to her tent. She thought she could grow accustomed to the silence. But she couldn't.

Just then she heard her husband draw back the fold on his side of the tent. Her hands moved quickly to arrange the evening meal. He would be tired from a day with the herdsmen. She understood that. But perhaps, with some refreshment, with some coaxing, they might try again to make their marriage fruitful.

Meet a Hero

"The one thing I desired more than anything else was a child. (See Genesis 17:1–18:15; 20:1–12.) But I was barren and had come to accept my fate—unable to provide my husband with offspring. Though God promised a child in my old age, I doubted. In fact, I laughed bitterly. Yet God kept His promise to me! I now have my child, and we will name him Isaac.

"God kept the promise He made to my husband, Abraham, even when it seemed impossible for Him to keep His promise. I have learned that with God anything is possible, including the birth of a promised child when it would be physically impossible. God makes endless impossibilities possible."

Surprises

Fun surprises come in all shapes and sizes. They consist of exciting news, colorfully wrapped packages, or unexpected visitors. Surprises often bring laughter and tears of joy and carry with them anticipation for another wonderful mystery. In the Bible reading, God surprises Abraham and Sarah with joyous but unbelievable news.

It is not shocking that He is able to perform the miracle of giving them a son. God abundantly provides for us, His children, and takes pleasure in blessing us. We, too, can enjoy the unforeseen surprises in our life. Share some of the surprises in your life.

Impossible Promise

9. Read Genesis 17:1–27. What does God promise Abraham? How does Abraham respond? Why does he respond this way? How does God respond to Abraham?

10. Read Genesis 18:15. Why did Sarah respond to God's promise in this way? What does God say in response to Sarah's reaction?

11. God fulfilled His promise to Abraham and Sarah. What event does the miraculous birth of this child foreshadow? (See Galatians 3:16.)

12. Read Genesis 21. How does Abraham respond to the fulfillment of God's promise? Sarah?

Miracle Child

13. The 18th-century philosopher David Hume delivered a devastating blow on the unsuspecting Church. From the observation of uniform laws of nature, Hume said, we can conclude that there is a uniform experience against the miraculous happening. That is, because of the order found in nature, miracles cannot occur. What sorts of problems with the Christian faith are caused by Hume's argument? How can we respond to this particular attack against the Christian faith?

14. Abraham and Sarah witnessed God miraculously fulfill His promise. What promise has God given us? How has this promise already been fulfilled? How is it yet to be fulfilled? (See Galatians 3:26–29.)

For This Week

- If you have the time, try to surprise someone with a special gift (card, letter, present, flowers, or a kind gesture).
- You would be surprised to see how far a smile can go. Can you spread some cheer to friends and strangers as you go about your daily business?

Closing Worship

Sing "My Faith Looks Trustingly" (*LW* 378).

My faith looks trustingly
To Christ of Calvary,
My Savior true!
Lord, hear me while I pray,
Take all my guilt away,
Strengthen in ev'ry way
My love for You!

May Your rich grace impart
Strength to my fainting heart,
My zeal inspire;
As You have died for me,
My love, adoringly,
Pure, warm, and changeless be,
A living fire!

While life's dark maze I tread
And griefs around me spread,
Oh, be my guide;
Make darkness turn to day,
Wipe sorrow's tears away,
Nor let me ever stray
From You aside.

When ends life's transient dream,
When death's cold, sullen stream
Rolls over me,
Blest Savior, then in love
Fear and distrust remove;
Oh, bear me safe above,
Redeemed and free!

To prepare for "Jacob and Esau," read Genesis 25:19–37:11.

Worldly Powers	Dates	Bible Heroes
Satan	Creation	Adam & Eve
Neo-Sumerian	2000 B.C.	Abraham & Sarah
	1980 B.C.	*Jacob & Esau*
Egypt, New Kingdom	1500 B.C.	Moses
Philistine Invasion	1000 B.C.	King David
Old Testament Ends	430 B.C.	
Romans	A.D. 27	Jesus Christ ✝

Cultural Setting

"The herdsmen must move the flocks to the north. Let them know."

"But the flocks to the east have not been moved for two days!" the younger brother protested.

The older brother glared. "Move the flocks to the *north*," he emphasized and turned to enter his tent.

The younger brother watched him go, helpless to protest further. Then he started walking north. He honored his brother but could not bring himself to like him. It had been weeks since they greeted one another with "Shalom."

His brother had all the advantages. He would inherit a double portion of the property. He would manage the affairs of the entire family to his advantage. He would bear the family name and titles. He belonged to God. As the firstfruits of marriage, his parents had offered him to the Ruler of all.

"Perhaps he will err," the younger brother schemed. "Perhaps he will dishonor the family and so disgrace himself that father will have to look to me." He had seen his older brother flirting with his father's concubine—a dangerous game. "Perhaps he will overstep his rights and visit her portion of the tent. Then I will have the birthright."

Meet a Hero

"Okay, so I wasn't an angel. Sure I deceived my father, Isaac, in order to win the birthright. But my brother, Esau, was willing to sell it to me for some bread and lentil stew. Hey, he was willing to sell what was rightfully his, and I was willing to take it.

"But to confirm my ownership of the birthright, I had to deceive my father. Convincing him that I was Esau took some doing! My mother and I decided that I would cook my father's favorite meal and cover my hands and neck with goatskins so that my father would think I was Esau. The plot to steal the birthright worked!

"Although Esau had earlier sold his birthright to me, when he realized what had happened, he was furious. There would be no reconciliation. I left my father and my mother, Rebekah, and went to live with my mother's brother, Laban. I found out quickly that Laban was capable of outsmarting even me. He made a promise that I could marry his daughter

Rachel; then he gave me his daughter Leah. After I agreed to work for Laban seven more years, he gave me Rachel for my wife.

"For many years I prospered. God continued to bless me, although I had done nothing to deserve His favor. Then, one day as I traveled back to the land of my fathers, I looked up and saw Esau coming with four hundred men. Fearing the safety of my family, I approached Esau, bowing down seven times. Incredibly, Esau ran to meet me and embraced me. Truly, God had performed yet another miracle in my life . . . His love and forgiveness had empowered Esau to love and forgive me."

Rivalry

Most of us can relate to sibling rivalry. The emotions that accompany such contention are far too familiar to many of us. This is also the case with Jacob and Esau throughout their younger years. Jacob continues to scale the ladder of strength and superiority. Esau, on the other hand, must helplessly watch his birthright and blessing being stolen from him. However, God has a plan for them and continues blessing them throughout the rest of their lives. God has a plan for you as well. Take time to talk with Him today about what your future holds.

Deception

15. In Genesis 27:36 Esau says, "Isn't he rightly named Jacob?" In the Hebrew language, Jacob's name means "grabber." In the following verses, how does he live up to his name?

a. 25:26, 33:

b. 27:18–29:

c. 32:26:

16. In Genesis 32:11–12 what does Jacob say to God?

17. Jacob held God to His word. What were the results of Jacob's faith in God's promises?

18. Did Esau have a right to carry a grudge? What attitude does he have when he finally meets his brother again?

19. What is Jacob's name changed to (Genesis 35:10–11)? How is this a fulfillment of God's promise to Abraham?

Hold to the Word

20. Have you ever been deceived by someone close to you? Did you retaliate?

21. In today's study we learned that Jacob held God to His word. What words has God given us that we can hold fast to? (See Titus 1:1–4.) How is this carried out in worship?

22. As a result of trusting God, Jacob prospered. What will be our reward for trusting God and His Word? Who is responsible for this faith? How is this faith nurtured? (See Romans 10:17.)

23. Is there anyone you haven't forgiven because they deceived you? How might you follow Esau's example—empowered by God's love for you in Jesus—and forgive them?

For This Week

- Call a sibling or close friend and let that person know how much he or she means to you.
- Pray for someone who has hurt you recently. Ask God to bless that individual with His grace, and pray that He will mend the pain and sorrow inflicting you.

Closing Worship

Pray together the Lord's Prayer.

To prepare for "Jacob and Rachel," read Genesis 29:9–30:24; 31:1–21.

Worldly Powers	Dates	Bible Heroes
Satan	Creation	Adam & Eve
Neo-Sumerian	2000 B.C.	Abraham & Sarah
	1876 B.C.	*Jacob & Rachel*
Egypt, New Kingdom	1500 B.C.	Moses
Philistine Invasion	1000 B.C.	King David
Old Testament Ends	430 B.C.	
Romans	A.D. 27	Jesus Christ ✝

Cultural Setting

The fine, bright veil accented her dark eyes but tickled her nose and chin. She smiled with anticipation. Soon her family would lead her with song from her father's tent to the tent of her bridegroom, her lord. "Thirty shekels," she thought. "Thirty silver shekels my father and bridegroom agreed. How dearly they value me! How many gifts my bridegroom gave my parents when they sealed the covenant! And why not? He is the firstborn son of my uncle, our dearest kin.

"I wonder what gifts my parents will leave with me at his tent? Perhaps a servant girl. Let a servant girl be among the gifts, a companion and helper from my father's household!"

Light flashed suddenly across her eyes as her mother opened the tent and entered.

"Soon you will stand quietly, respectfully, by your beloved," her mother whispered at her ear. "He will announce for all to hear, 'She is my wife and I am her husband, from this day forever.'"

Meet a Hero

"Have you ever loved someone so much that you were willing to do anything and everything to prove it? That is how much I loved Rachel. From my youth I knew that she was the woman I wanted to spend my entire life with. But then her father, Laban, had different ideas. Boy, did he make it difficult to fulfill my dream of marrying his daughter. I promised to work for Laban for seven years in order to have the privilege of marrying his daughter. The seven years seemed like only days to me, because I loved Rachel so much. Then, on the night of my wedding, Laban pulled a bait and switch. He gave me his older daughter, Leah, and I slept with her.

"When I realized the next day that I had slept with Leah instead of Rachel, I confronted Laban with his deception. Laban told me that the custom was to first marry off the older daughter prior to the younger. Laban then told me I could work for seven more years for him in exchange for Rachel. Although tough to believe, my love for Rachel motivated me to work those seven years.

"Rachel became jealous of her sister Leah because she was not able to bear me children. Finally, Rachel did conceive and bear me a son, Joseph."

Working Man

Saturday afternoon was the dreaded time in our house—for me anyway. That was the special, wonderful day when chores had to be completed. Even though I was paid for my hard work, I still took shortcuts. I discovered that the toilets looked just as clean when I meticulously wiped them with a dry rag instead of cleaning solution and a wet sponge. In spite of my dishonest timesaving abilities, I was still given an allowance. Hard work is not easy, but it does pay off in the end. Jacob devoted 14 years of his life to Laban in order to have Rachel as his wife. Jacob's job was not always easy, but he worked diligently in order to receive his long-awaited prize. How does Jacob's work ethic provide an incentive to strive harder during challenging circumstances?

The Bargain

24. Read Genesis 29:9–30. What agreement with Laban in exchange for work does Jacob come to? What happens after Jacob fulfills his end of the bargain? Then what happens? How did Jacob feel about Rachel?

25. In Genesis 30:2, Jacob answers Rachel's plea for children. He says, "Am I in the place of God, who has kept you from having children?" What is the irony of this statement in light of what you know of Jacob's personality? How does Rachel take matters into her own hands?

26. Read 31:1–21. What did Rachel do before she and Jacob left her father? How is this in conflict with Jacob's faith? What does Jacob do to reconcile this conflict?

The Blessings

27. Jacob and Rachel have a small part of the bigger picture of the Christian faith. What is Jacob and Rachel's role in the Christian faith?

28. God blesses His human creatures with relationships. We especially see God's blessings in our spouse and children. What relationships has God blessed you with? (See Titus 3:4–7.) How is Jacob's love for Rachel a model for the submission and love spouses have for each other?

Closing Worship

Sing stanzas 1, 2, and 3 of "For All the Saints" (*LW* 191).

For all the saints who from their labors rest,
All who by faith before the world confessed,
Your name, O Jesus, be forever blest.
Alleluia! Alleluia!

You were their rock, their fortress, and their might;
You, Lord, their captain in the well-fought fight;
You, in the darkness drear, their one true light.
Alleluia! Alleluia!

Oh, may Your soldiers, faithful, true, and bold,
Fight as the saints who nobly fought of old
And win with them the victor's crown of gold.
Alleluia! Alleluia!

To prepare for "Joseph and His Brothers," read Genesis 37:1–36; 39:1–50:26.

Worldly Powers	Dates	Bible Heroes
Satan	Creation	Adam & Eve
Neo-Sumerian	2000 B.C.	Abraham & Sarah
	1915 B.C.	*Joseph*
Egypt, New Kingdom	1500 B.C.	Moses
Philistine Invasion	1000 B.C.	King David
Old Testament Ends	430 B.C.	
Romans	A.D. 27	Jesus Christ ✝

Cultural Setting

"Tamp. Tamp," whispered the loom as he drove the weft together with a stick. He quickly slid the shuttle between the linen strands and tamped the thread down again. As his arms worked the loom, the goat-hair garment he wore nibbled and itched his flesh. Its gray appearance marked him as a slave.

The pure white cloth on the loom made the young man dream of soft lambs' wool spun by his mother's nimble fingers. He remembered his father working the white wool back and forth on a loom and tamping it tight. He had worn the coat his father made. It ran down his lithe arms to the wrists, down his legs to the ankles. It blocked the sun's heat and felt smooth against his skin. But the raiders had torn it. "One of their sons must wear it now," he imagined.

"Tamp. Tamp." The loom whispered and the young slave's dream unraveled.

Meet a Hero

"The truth is, my father did show favoritism to me over my brothers. Now as I look back, I understand why my brothers grew to hate me so. But still, did they really have to sell me into slavery and then lie to my father, saying I had been killed?

"God continued to demonstrate His love for me even as I experienced the depths of despair as a slave in Egypt. And He gave me this incredible ability to share the meaning of dreams. The use of that gift enabled me to be elevated within the Egyptian government so that I could help my people, my family. I was able to warn the pharaoh of drought, and the Egyptians were able to store food enough for all the people during a time when neighboring countries experienced famine.

"Famine finally brought my brothers to Egypt. Jacob sent my brothers to Egypt, for he had heard that there was food in Egypt. When I first saw my brothers, I didn't disclose myself to them. In spite of what my brothers had done to me, God enabled me to love and to forgive them.

"Throughout the troubles and hardships I faced, God was at work. He directed my life. He was able to use the wickedness of my brothers to bring about good for them and me. His great love for me ultimately empowered me to love them."

Action

Are you familiar with the phrase "actions speak louder than words"? It is played in songs, chanted on the playground, and discussed among college students over lunch. How seriously do you take this thought? For Joseph, these words hit home. He was hated by his brothers, forced to become a slave, betrayed by Potiphar's wife, but blessed by God. By God's guiding and through Joseph's actions, a nation was saved and a family was reunited. How can you be confident of God's love when everything seems to go wrong?

Reactions

29. How do Joseph's brothers react to his dreams (Genesis 37:5–7, 9)? How do the brothers treat Joseph after he tells them his dreams?

30. Read Genesis 37:12–36. As the oldest brother, Reuben had authority over all the brothers. What did Reuben have the power to do? How does Reuben act like a coward? How does Reuben sin against Joseph and his father, Jacob?

31. In Genesis 42:22 Reuben exclaims, "Now we must give an accounting for [Joseph's] blood." In Genesis 42:37, what does he do instead of give an accounting for Joseph's blood?

32. When Joseph finally disclosed himself, his brothers were terrified (Genesis 45:3). How does Joseph deal with his brothers? Joseph doesn't blame his brothers, but rather he tells them, "God sent me ahead of you to preserve for you a remnant on earth and to save your lives by a great deliverance" (Genesis 45:7). What is this ultimately referring to?

Dreams

33. While waiting for his dream to be fulfilled, Joseph worked without a grudge. How is Joseph's attitude toward the work before him a model for how we work at our vocations? Joseph's hard work was done in the shadow of a promise. How is our work done in the shadow of a promise?

34. Reuben was the representative head of his brothers. He sinned in that capacity: halfheartedly attempting to save Joseph (Genesis 37:22), placing blame on his brothers (Genesis 42:22), and joining his brothers in blaming their misfortune on God (Genesis 42:28). We can find those sins in our lives today. Have you ever taken your responsibilities halfheartedly? Have you ever blamed your misfortunes on others? on God? Explain.

35. Joseph had a dream from the Lord. Connected with that dream was a promise. Throughout his life Joseph knew that one day this dream would be fulfilled. Read Hebrews 11:21–22, 39–40. What promise have we been given? When will it be fulfilled?

For This Week

- Make a list of the negative, difficult events and the positive, uplifting events that you have experienced this week. Focus on the positive events and offer a prayer of thanksgiving to God for His forgiving love.
- Find a creative way (a love note, a phone call, an e-mail) to remind someone of God's love in Jesus Christ.

Closing Worship

Sing "Sing Praise to God, the Highest Good" (*LW* 452).

Sing praise to God, the highest good,
The author of creation,
The God of love who understood
Our need for His salvation.
With healing balm our souls He fills
And ev'ry faithless murmur stills:
To God all praise and glory!

What God's almighty pow'r had made,
In mercy He is keeping;
By morning glow or evening shade
His eye is never sleeping;
Within the kingdom of His might
All things are just and good and right:
To God all praise and glory!

We sought the Lord in our distress;
O God, in mercy hear us.
Our Savior saw our helplessness
And came with peace to cheer us.
For this we thank and praise the Lord,
Who is by one and all adored:
To God all praise and glory!

All who confess Christ's holy name,
Give God the praise and glory.
Let all who know His pow'r proclaim
Aloud the wondrous story.
Cast ev'ry idol from its throne,
For God is God, and He alone:
To God all praise and glory!

To prepare for "Mary and Joseph," read Matthew 1:18–25; Luke 1:26–55; 2:1–52.

Worldly Powers	Dates	Bible Heroes
Satan	Creation	Adam & Eve
Neo-Sumerian	2000 B.C.	Abraham & Sarah
Egypt, New Kingdom	1500 B.C.	Moses
Philistine Invasion	1000 B.C.	King David
Old Testament Ends	430 B.C.	
	5 B.C.	*Mary & Joseph*
Romans	A.D. 27	Jesus Christ ✝

Cultural Setting

His trembling hand set the reed pen down. He stared blankly at the parchment, imagining the words. The opinion of the liberal rabbi Hillel appealed to him. Hillel argued from Deuteronomy 24 that a man could divorce his wife for any cause. He could simply and easily abandon her to her father's house. However, conservative rabbi Shammai read the passage differently. He argued that this passage referred only to marital unfaithfulness as grounds for divorce. Which was right?

To complicate matters further, they had not yet consummated the marriage. They were betrothed but did not yet live together. His silver shekels now clinked in her father's leather pouch. His presents rested at their household. To divorce her now, when everyone anticipated the wedding procession and celebration, would be extremely awkward.

For a moment his anger turned away from the girl. "How very young she is. How lasting a shame will follow her because her father gave her too much freedom. His fault!" he thought as he lifted the reed pen and examined its ink-stained tip. This point would pierce the hearts of all, if he scribed the words.

Meet a Hero

"Impossible! Why would God choose me? What had I done to deserve to become the mother of the Savior? Impossible! I would give birth to a child, but I was still a virgin. Impossible! God would enable Joseph to continue to love me and remain faithful to his promise to marry me in spite of a pregnancy that for all intents and purposes was highly suspicious.

"What I learned from my experience is that God is able to make the impossible possible! Why would He do this? Because He loved me, who does not deserve His love, with a love that is gracious. Because He loved all people so much that He would send a Savior. My child, Jesus, would eventually suffer and die on a cross for my sins and the sins of all people. Joseph and I and all people would receive an incredible gift because of Jesus—the gift of forgiveness of sins and eternal life."

Trust

"Trust me." I remember hearing that phrase as a child hiking through unfamiliar territory, as a teenager preparing for high school, and as a college student stressed out about the major projects looming ahead. My parents knew that those words would bring comfort to my fears and uncertainties. I knew, even when I was stubborn, that they were telling the truth: everything would work out and I could trust them. Our heavenly Father offers us the same advice. We do not need to worry about our future because God is in control (Jeremiah 29:11; Romans 8). God sent angels to Mary and Joseph to deliver the Good News about the birth of the Savior and through His Word proclaimed by the angel empowered them to trust Him. We continually turn our backs on God and try to solve problems with our own strength. How has His intervention during past difficulties revealed to you the need to trust Him now?

Expectant

36. Read Luke 1:26–38. How did the angel greet Mary? Why did this greeting trouble Mary? How does Mary respond to the angel's news? What does this tell you about Mary?

37. Human reason says that a virgin cannot give birth. What does the angel Gabriel say concerning what is and isn't possible?

38. In the Magnificat (Luke 1:46–55) Mary says that all nations will consider her blessed. What is there about God that enabled her to say these things?

39. Matthew 1:19 says that Joseph was a righteous man. In Matthew 1:18–25, what evidence is there of Joseph's righteousness?

The Great News

40. It has been said that reason is what separates humans from the animals. Yet miraculous events are unexplainable by human reason alone. Could it be said that reason is what separates us from God (Genesis 6:5; Romans 1:21–23)?

41. Mary and Joseph are wonderful examples of passive submission to God's revelation. In response to Gabriel's message, Mary said, "May it be to me as you have said" (Luke 1:38). After Joseph was told about Mary's pregnancy in a dream, he "did what the angel of the Lord had commanded him" (Matthew 1:24). Compare and contrast God's gift of faith to you and the account of Mary and Joseph.

42. What happened through Mary is perhaps the greatest event in history. List some things you can do to be a messenger of this great news.

For This Week

- Test your ability to trust. Offer your problems to the Lord and trust that He will take care of them by giving you the guidance you need.
- Pray for missionaries, pastors, and teachers who entrust their lives to God and His promises. Ask God to carry them safely through troublesome times.

Closing Worship

Sing together "I Am Trusting You, Lord Jesus" (*LW* 408).

I am trusting You, Lord Jesus,
Trusting only You;
Trusting You for full salvation,
Free and true.

I am trusting You for pardon;
At Your feet I bow,
For Your grace and tender mercy
Trusting now.

I am trusting You for cleansing
In the crimson flood;
Trusting You to make me holy
By Your blood.

I am trusting You to guide me;
You alone shall lead,
Ev'ry day and hour supplying
All my need.

I am trusting You for power;
You can never fail.
Words which You Yourself shall give me
Must prevail.

I am trusting You, Lord Jesus;
Never let me fall.
I am trusting You forever
And for all.

Leader Guide

Leaders, please note the different abilities of your class members. Some will easily find the Bible passages listed in this study. Others will need assistance. To make participation easier, team up members of the class. For example, if a question asks you to look up several passages, assign one passage to one group, the second to another, and so forth. Divide up the work! Let participants present the different answers they discover.

Introduce each biblical character with the following tools:

Chart helps students locate the Bible character in world history and in relation to major biblical figures.

Setting provides students with a cultural setting of what life was like for the people of that day (this section is *not* intended to directly describe the biblical character).

Meet a Hero summarizes the portion of the Bible that will be studied so that people who are new to Bible study can "catch up" with mature Bible students as they discuss the Bible character together. To spice up the lesson, invite a dynamic member of your class to deliver this character monologue in a dramatic fashion.

Each topic then divides into three easy-to-use sections:

Focus introduces key concepts that will be discovered.

Inform guides the participants into Scripture to uncover truth about how God made the Bible character into a hero and redeems all people through Christ.

Connect enables participants to apply that which is learned in Scripture to their lives and provides them an opportunity to formulate and articulate a defense of a key doctrine.

Conclude each session by discussing **For This Week**, which provides participants with practical suggestions for extending the theme of the lesson out of the classroom and into the world, and by using the **Worship** suggestions.

Adam and Eve

(Genesis 1:27–3:24)

Objectives

By the power of the Holy Spirit working through God's Word, we will

- describe the cause of sin and its consequences;
- explain how, in spite of our disobedience, God continues to bless us;
- affirm the fulfillment of God's promise to Adam and Eve and its ramifications for us.

Opening Worship

O God, whose almighty power is made known chiefly in showing mercy and pity, grant us the fullness of Your grace that we may be partakers of Your heavenly treasures; through our Lord Jesus Christ, Your Son, who lives and reigns with You and the Holy Spirit, one God, now and forever. Amen.

Cultural Setting and Meet a Hero

Have participants read these two sections silently or ask volunteers to read them aloud. Consider having a class member act out "Meet a Hero" as a dramatic monologue.

A Promise for All (Focus)

Adam and Eve sinned against the Lord by disobeying His commands. Because of their sin they were removed from the fullness of God's blessings. Our sin results in the same separation from God. God promised our first parents and all following generations to put an end to sin and death. Christ's death on the cross was the fulfillment of this promise. God has brought us back into a right relationship with Him.

Invite volunteers to read aloud "A Promise for All." Focus on the promise of salvation that has been given to us. Encourage the participants to think critically about the relationships they have been blessed with (spouse, children, parents, etc.). The best relationship we can be thankful for is our relationship with Christ. He sacrificed Himself for us so we could live with Him.

Perfect Marriage (Inform)

Have the participants read through Genesis 2:15–3:24.

1. God formed Eve from Adam because there wasn't a suitable helper for him. God saw that it was not good for Adam to be alone. He caused Adam to fall into a deep sleep. While he was sleeping, God removed one of Adam's ribs and formed Eve. Adam's first reaction to seeing Eve was one of amazement. Adam said, "This is now bone of my bones and flesh of my flesh; she shall be called 'woman,' for she was taken out of man" (Genesis 2:23). God created Eve to be Adam's partner in taking care of the garden. Men and women are meant to be together as partners and co-workers. Prior to the fall, Adam and Eve's relationship was sinless. They enjoyed each other's company and cared for one another as much as themselves. It wouldn't be until they fell into sin that their relationship would be filled with conflict.

2. The actions of Adam and Eve are anything but heroic! God told Adam that he was not to eat from the "tree of the knowledge of good and evil" (Genesis 2:17). When Eve was tempted by the serpent, she added to God's commands by saying that she and her husband were not allowed to even touch it. The result of eating from the tree would be death. The serpent told Eve that whoever ate from the tree would not die, but rather they would be like God. Faced with the serpent's enticing lie of acquiring wisdom, Eve looked at the fruit in the tree, saw that it looked good, and ate from the tree.

3. After Adam answered God in the garden and disclosed why he was hiding, God asked him how he knew he was naked. Adam dodged God's question by telling God what Eve had done. He did not answer God's question. Instead, knowing that he had sinned, he immediately blamed Eve and ultimately blamed God. Accusingly, Adam said, "The woman You put here with me—she gave me some fruit from the tree" (Genesis 3:12). Adam knew he had disobeyed God, and in fear he sought to place the blame on someone else.

4. After Adam and Eve disobeyed, the Lord cursed Eve. He pronounced that she would have great pain in her childbearing and she would be subject to her husband (her husband would "rule over" her [Genesis 3:16]). On account of Adam, God cursed the ground and proclaimed that man would spend his days working for basic human needs. God also announced that man would experience death. God cursed the serpent. But what was a curse for the serpent is a blessing for us. God said, "I will put enmity between you and the woman, and between your

offspring and hers; He will crush your head, and you will strike His heel" (Genesis 3:15). Though the people of the world (Eve's offspring) would encounter many struggles with the serpent (the devil), eventually one of Eve's offspring would emerge as a hero, to deliver the final blow to the devil's work. This points us to the cross of Christ, where sin was dealt with once and for all (John 19:30; Hebrews 13:20). Although Christ died on the cross, He would rise again announcing victory over the curse of sin, death, and the devil. The promise delivered to Adam and Eve, our representative parents, is for all people.

Our Inheritance (Connect)

5. The Lutheran theologian Edward Koehler defines original sin: "The sin of our first parents was of disastrous consequence not only to them personally, but also to all their offspring, inasmuch as the guilt of their first transgression is imputed, and the corruption of their nature is transmitted, to all their children" (*A Summary of Christian Doctrine,* CPH 1971). In other words, just as we inherit certain physical traits from our parents, we also inherit the same willful disobedience against God. The consequence of this condition is eternal death. Regardless of how pious and holy we may live our lives, our sinful condition warrants God's justice—death.

6. Answers will vary. Adam ultimately blamed God for his sin. Some theologians attribute the cause of sin to God. They argue that God has to will something in order for it to be. Therefore, God must have willed the fall in order for it to have happened. But in Genesis 3:17 God assigns blame to Adam and Eve by saying, "Because you listened to your wife and ate from the tree about which I commanded you, 'You must not eat of it.'" Concerning the cause of sin, we are limited to the words of Scripture. According to Scripture, it was man's will that chose to disobey God. To say more—such as that God foreknew the fall, therefore He must have willed it—goes beyond the teachings of Scripture (Psalm 5:4–5).

7. In Genesis 3:15 God curses the serpent but offers a promise to all people. A woman's offspring would crush the work of the serpent. That is, this heroic offspring would undo sin and death. See also the answer to question 4.

8. Answers will vary. Though death's threats continue, God's grace and promise overflow to us in Christ. His resurrection is our guarantee of eternal life.

For This Week

Urge participants to complete one or both of the suggested activities for the week.

Closing Worship

Sing in unison stanzas 1, 3, and 5 of "Jesus Sinners Will Receive" (*LW* 229).

Abraham and Sarah

(Genesis 17:1–18:15; 20:1–21:12)

Objectives

By the power of the Holy Spirit working through God's Word, we will
- describe the promise God made to Abraham and Sarah;
- explain the fulfillment of God's promise to Abraham and Sarah in spite of their unbelief;
- confess God's promise and its fulfillment to us.

Opening Worship

O God, the Protector of all who trust in You, without whom nothing is strong and holy, increase and multiply Your mercy on us that with You as our Ruler and Guide we may so pass through things temporal that we lose not the things eternal; through Jesus Christ, Your Son, our Lord, who lives and reigns with You and the Holy Spirit, one God, now and forever. Amen.

Cultural Setting and Meet a Hero

Have participants read these two sections silently or ask volunteers to read them aloud. Consider having a class member act out "Meet a Hero" as a dramatic monologue.

Surprises (Focus)

How many times do we say we will do something only to forget about it? Not only do we forget our promises, we ignore and forget about God's commandments. Forgetting God's commands is not like forgetting to do something for a friend. Failing to keep God's Law results in eternal death. Knowing our sinful condition, God made a unique promise to us. Through His Son's death on the cross, God kept His promise to give us eternal life. Christ's life, death, and resurrection fulfilled God's promise to us.

Read this paragraph aloud. Point out the surprise and miracle of Isaac to Abraham and Sarah. Ask volunteers to discuss some of their favorite surprises. Allow them to reflect upon God's gifts in their lives and the surprises yet to come.

Impossible Promise (Inform)

9. God promised Abraham that he would be the father of many nations. He also promised him that his wife would bear a son in her old age. Abraham responds by falling facedown in laughter. He did not believe that Sarah could give birth in her old age. The thought of it was absurd. God responded to Abraham by reaffirming His promise. Even in unbelief, God displays patience toward Abraham.

10. Sarah responds to God's promise in a similar manner to Abraham. From the tent she overheard Abraham's conversation and, in disbelief, laughed to herself. God responded to Sarah's unbelief by asking Abraham, "Is anything too hard for the LORD?" (Genesis 18:14). That is, who were Abraham and Sarah to doubt what God was capable of performing?

11. God fulfilled His promise to Abraham and Sarah. Isaac's birth was a miracle. This event foreshadows the miraculous birth of Christ. When Mary asked the angel Gabriel how it was that she was pregnant, the angel responded by stating, "Nothing is impossible with God" (Luke 1:37).

12. Abraham responded to God's blessing by having Isaac circumcised in accordance with the covenant God had established with him earlier. Sarah responds by laughing. This time the laughter was not from disbelief, but out of joy. God's promise to Abraham and Sarah was finally fulfilled. God confirms His promise to us today through the "circumcision" of the New Testament: Baptism (Colossians 2:1–14).

Miracle Child (Connect)

13. David Hume's argument against the miraculous lays the groundwork for modern skepticism. According to Hume, miracles such as the incarnation and resurrection of Christ are impossible. The Christian faith is grounded in the miracles of Christ's birth and resurrection. Even though Hume lived about 250 years ago, his skepticism is still prevalent today. When Abraham displayed skepticism, the Lord asked, "Is anything too hard for the LORD?" (Genesis 18:14).

14. God has promised us eternal life in heaven. Christ's death and resurrection fulfilled this promise. When we come to the end of our life or the Lord returns, He will fulfill this promise for us. Given the fulfill-

ment of the promise in Christ's death and resurrection, we can be certain of the future fulfillment (1 Corinthians 15:20).

For This Week

Encourage group members to complete one or both of the suggested activities.

Closing Worship

Sing in unison "My Faith Looks Trustingly" (*LW* 378).

Jacob and Esau

(Genesis 25:19–37:11)

Objectives

By the power of the Holy Spirit working through God's Word, we will
- describe the tension between Jacob and Esau;
- explain how God healed Jacob and Esau's relationship;
- affirm how God keeps His promise to heal His people.

Opening Worship

Almighty, everlasting God, whose Son has assured forgiveness of sins and deliverance from eternal death, strengthen us by Your Holy Spirit that our faith in Christ increase daily and we hold fast the hope that we shall not die but fall asleep and on the Last Day be raised to eternal life; through Jesus Christ, our Lord. Amen.

Cultural Setting and Meet a Hero

Have participants read these two sections silently or ask volunteers to read them aloud. Consider having a class member act out "Meet a Hero" as a dramatic monologue.

Rivalry (Focus)

We are often deceived by others, but even more so we deceive ourselves. We ignore God's commandments and think that we have a better way. Our way leads only to death and damnation. God never deceives us. His promise of salvation was completed at Calvary's cross. Jesus' life, death, and resurrection were for us and cannot be undone.

Ask a volunteer to read aloud the opening paragraph. Allow time for participants to discuss what they have read as a group, and give them personal time to talk with God. If time permits and if Bible study members are willing, have them talk about their prayer requests.

Deception (Inform)

15. Jacob was always "grabbing" for things. In Genesis 25:26 and 33 Jacob came out of his mother's womb grabbing the heel of his twin brother, Esau. Some years later, after Esau returned from a hunting trip, Jacob conned his older brother into selling his birthright in exchange for some food. In 27:18–29 Jacob, with the help of his mother, Rebekah, deceived his father and Esau. Jacob pretended to be Esau, and Isaac gave him the blessing he had reserved for Esau. In 32:26 Jacob wrestled with God. After wrestling all night and with his hipbone out of its socket, Jacob would not let go of the man until He blessed him. Jacob received the Lord's blessing.

16. Jacob asks the Lord to save him. Jacob didn't simply plea for the Lord's intercession, but rather he holds God to His word. Jacob "reminds" God of the promise He had made previously with Abraham and his children.

17. When news reached Jacob that his brother was near, he was very afraid. But Jacob remembered the promise the Lord had made. Jacob was blessed for his faith. Esau had long since forgiven Jacob for what he had done, and the two brothers were reunited.

18. Esau had a right to be angry at his brother's schemes, but the Lord had blessed Esau. When Esau finally saw Jacob, he ran to Jacob without any vengeful hesitation.

19. Jacob's name was changed to Israel. The nation of Israel was to be a nation of God's people. God's promise to Abraham was beginning to be fulfilled through Isaac and then Jacob. Jacob had his own children. One would be in the lineage of King David, and even farther down the family lineage, Jesus, the promised Messiah.

Hold to the Word (Connect)

20. Answers will vary. Keep the participants from straying too far from the topic.

21. God has told us in Scripture that the work of redemption is complete. Through Christ's life, death, and resurrection our sins have been forgiven. In worship we begin by confessing our sins, and the pastor responds by proclaiming the forgiveness Jesus won for us. The Absolution pronounces us free from sin, death, and the devil. Answers may vary slightly. Participants might also focus on the words spoken during the Sacraments, where God's Word gives the visible elements their

power. The Sacraments offer us visible assurance of our forgiveness and the hope for eternal life.

22. Through the water and the Word of Baptism, God gives us His Holy Spirit. In the visible bread and wine of the Lord's Supper, Christ gives us His body and blood for the forgiveness of sins. In these physical ways, the Lord guarantees our physical resurrection from the dead.

23. Answers will vary.

For This Week

Encourage participants to complete one or both of the suggested activities.

Closing Worship

Pray together the Lord's Prayer.

Jacob and Rachel

(Genesis 29:9–30:24; 31:1–21; 35:1–5)

Objectives

By the power of the Holy Spirit working through God's Word, we will

- describe the result of Jacob's patience;
- explain Jacob and Rachel's role in God's plan from eternity;
- describe how God's plan of salvation relates to and affects you.

Opening Worship

Grant us, Lord, the Spirit to think and do always such things as are pleasing in Your sight that we, who without You cannot do anything that is good, may by You be enabled to live according to Your will; through Jesus Christ, Your Son, our Lord, who lives and reigns with You and the Holy Spirit, one God, now and forever. Amen.

Cultural Setting and Meet a Hero

Have participants read these two sections silently or ask volunteers to read them aloud. Consider having a class member act out "Meet a Hero" as a dramatic monologue.

Working Man (Focus)

God demands that we live according to His standards, but we fail to live up to them. The consequence of failing to meet God's standards is eternal death. In spite of our failure, God sent His Son to keep His Law in our place. Christ's death on the cross frees us from eternal punishment. On account of this, we live in anticipation of our eternal inheritance.

Ask a volunteer to read the opening paragraph. As humorous as the story is, focus on our sinful nature and the sins we commit. Challenge each Bible study member to reevaluate her or his work ethic and consider striving harder to accomplish monotonous tasks. Life on this earth is only temporal! That is a blessing and God's sustaining Holy Spirit can give us the incentive to "push ourselves" until God relieves us and invites us to rest with Him eternally.

The Bargain (Inform)

Have participants read Genesis 29:9–30:24; 31:1–21; 35:1–5.

24. In exchange for seven years of work, Laban agreed to give his daughter Rachel in marriage to Jacob. From the moment Jacob laid his eyes on her, he loved her. The seven years he spent working for Laban went by fast. After the marriage feast was over, Laban substituted Leah for Rachel. Jacob didn't notice it until they had consummated their marriage. When he noticed what had been done, he confronted Laban. Laban responded by saying that the local custom was for the oldest daughter to be married off first. After Jacob held Laban to his word, Laban gave Rachel to him in exchange for seven more years of work.

25. Jacob was a "grabber." He came out of his mother's womb grabbing his brother's heel. He seized the opportunity to take advantage of Esau's momentary weakness and secured his birthright. He even deceived his father into giving him the family blessing, which was intended for Esau. His most prominent act of "grabbing" came when he wrestled with God and would not let go of Him until he was blessed. Jacob took advantage of situations. Instead of patiently waiting for blessings, he took matters into his own hands. After meeting Laban, Jacob becomes more patient. He waited for seven years and a week to be married to Rachel. When Rachel begs for a child, he ironically says, "Am I in the place of God . . . " Rachel took matters into her own hands when she had Jacob father a child with her maidservant Bilhah.

26. When Jacob was preparing to leave Laban, Rachel stole her father's gods. Rachel still retained her pagan beliefs in spite of being married to Jacob. In Genesis 35:1–5, Jacob ordered his family to get rid of their pagan idols. After they gave up their idolatry, Jacob had his whole family purified, and they became the children of Israel.

The Blessings (Connect)

27. Through Jacob and Rachel's son Joseph, the Israelites would be saved from famine. From this remnant would come forth the promised Messiah.

28. Answers will vary. Jacob demonstrates the same love for Rachel that Christ has for His people. Christ loves us unconditionally as Jacob loved Rachel from first glance. Christ sacrificed Himself so that we might be in a right relationship with God, just as Jacob sacrificed

seven years and a week to be married to Rachel. Jacob's love for Rachel came unconditionally, as does Christ's love for us.

For This Week

Urge participants to complete one or more of the suggested activities.

Closing Worship

Sing in unison stanzas 1, 2, and 3 of "For All the Saints" (*LW* 191).

Joseph and His Brothers

(Genesis 37:1–36; 39:1–50:26)

Objectives

By the power of the Holy Spirit working through God's Word, we will

- describe the events that occurred between Joseph and his brothers;
- explain how God used Joseph's enslavement to serve a greater good;
- consider how God has released us from our enslavement to sin.

Opening Worship

O God, without whose blessing we are not able to please You, mercifully grant that Your Holy Spirit may in all things direct and govern our hearts; through Jesus Christ, Your Son, our Lord, who lives and reigns with You and the Holy Spirit, one God, now and forever. Amen.

Cultural Setting and Meet a Hero

Have participants read these two sections silently or ask volunteers to read them aloud. Consider having a class member act out "Meet a Hero" as a dramatic monologue.

Action (Focus)

We often fail to treat our family members as we should, but this is but a symptom of a deeper problem. We sin not because we occasionally slip; we sin because of who we are—slaves to sin. Instead of receiving our due punishment, we are set free. Christ's life, death, and resurrection paid our ransom price. We have been set free.

God gave His Son as the ultimate sacrifice so we could spend eternity with Him. Realize that God knows what He is doing and will give you the strength that is desperately needed when everything seems to go wrong.

Reactions (Inform)

Have the participants read Genesis 37:1–36 and 42:1–45:28.

29. After Joseph told his brothers his dreams, they "hated him all the more" (Genesis 37:5). They responded sarcastically to Joseph's dreams. After Joseph disclosed his dreams, Joseph's father, Jacob, rebuked him as well. Jacob asks, "Will your mother and I and your brothers actually come and bow down to the ground before you?" (Genesis 37:10). Even though Jacob was initially angry about Joseph's dreams, he kept them in mind. After Joseph's dreams, his brothers' jealousy turned into hate. Their hate led them to plot Joseph's death.

30. Reuben tried to save Joseph from his brothers' hands. Instead of killing him, Reuben ordered them to throw Joseph into a cistern. He planned on rescuing him later. Reuben had the power to order Joseph immediately released, but instead he compromises in the face of peer pressure. Reuben's plan to rescue Joseph failed. While he was waiting to bring Joseph back to Jacob, the brothers sold him into slavery. Reuben sinned against his father as well as Joseph. His father gave Reuben authority, which he did not use because of fear. Reuben was responsible for Joseph, but out of fear and peer pressure he let his brothers sell Joseph into slavery.

31. Rather then confessing his sin to his father, Reuben puts his own sons' lives on the line. Ironically, Reuben says, "Entrust him to my care, and I will bring him back" (Genesis 42:37). Reuben tries to make things right by requesting that Benjamin be placed in his care. Instead of confessing, Reuben prolongs his and his brothers' sin against Joseph. He would have been free of guilt had he asked for forgiveness years earlier.

32. Joseph deals kindly with his brothers. He had forgiven them; consequently, he was able to see God's purposes behind all that had happened to him. Joseph's words in Genesis 45:7 foreshadow the coming of Christ. From Jacob's family would come the promised Messiah who would save our lives "by a great deliverance" (Genesis 45:7). This great deliverance culminated in Christ's death and resurrection.

Dreams (Connect)

33. In spite of his situation, Joseph worked to the best of his ability. As a slave and a prisoner, Joseph worked without compromise and without a grudge. Joseph knew of God's promises to Israel (i.e., God would provide for them). Joseph is an exemplary model for us. Regardless of our station in life, God has placed us there for a reason. When we work to the best of our ability without complaint, we glorify God. We live in

the shadow of a fulfilled promise. Christ's death and resurrection give us hope, which cannot be taken away.

34. Answers will vary.

35. We constantly find ourselves blaming God and others for the situations we find ourselves in. In spite of this, God has given us a promise. He promises not only to be with us in our earthly journey, but through Christ He promises to keep us throughout all eternity. We can live and work with peace, knowing God keeps His promises and will keep His promises to us.

For This Week

Urge participants to complete one or both of the suggested activities.

Closing Worship

Sing in unison "Sing Praise to God, the Highest Good" (*LW* 452).

Mary and Joseph

(Matthew 1:18–25; Luke 1:26–55; 2:1–52)

Objectives

By the power of the Holy Spirit working through God's Word, we will

- describe how Mary and Joseph believed in God's Word;
- explain how God uses normal circumstances to accomplish what seems to be impossible;
- affirm the consequences of what God accomplished through Mary and Joseph.

Opening Worship

Stir up Your power, O Lord, and come among us with great might; and because we are sorely hindered by our sins, let Your bountiful grace and mercy speedily help and deliver us; through Jesus Christ, our Lord, who lives and reigns with You and the Holy Spirit, one God, now and forever. Amen.

Cultural Setting and Meet a Hero

Have participants read these two sections silently or ask volunteers to read them aloud. Consider having a class member act out "Meet a Hero" as a dramatic monologue.

Trust (Focus)

We receive the promise of salvation in the Word and at our Baptism. Yet our faith is often weak. Our weak faith is a consequence of sin—the sin of placing limits on what God can do. Christ's death on the cross accomplished the "impossible." Through the death of one man, all of humankind's sins are forgiven. God sends us the Holy Spirit to instill and strengthen our faith.

Have a volunteer read the paragraph aloud, and discuss the main idea of trusting. Work as a large group or in smaller groups and discuss the question. Emphasize the importance of trusting God for all things.

Answers will vary. Christ's faithfulness to us is a reassurance of His love. He holds our interests in His hands and desires us to prosper.

54

He has brought His children out of tribulation before and continues to do so.

Expectant (Inform)

Have participants read Luke 1:26–55; 2:1–52; Matthew 1:18–25.

36. The angel Gabriel appeared to Mary and said, "Greetings, you who are highly favored! The Lord is with you" (Luke 1:28). Mary was confused with Gabriel's words, for this was not a normal greeting in Nazareth. Mary also expressed fear in the presence of the angel Gabriel. After Gabriel announces that Mary was to give birth to a son, she responds by asking how it could be that a virgin would give birth. The angel explained to her that the Holy Spirit would come upon her and conceive a child in her womb. The angel also gives evidence to Mary that God was able to do miraculous things (e.g., Elizabeth's pregnancy in spite of the fact that she was barren). Mary simply responds in submission to God: "I am the Lord's servant. . . . May it be to me as you have said" (Luke 1:38).

37. When Mary asked the angel how a virgin could give birth, the angel Gabriel answered, "For nothing is impossible with God" (Genesis 1:37).

38. Mary was to give birth to the promised Messiah. Through Him the sins of all nations would be paid. Mary contained the divine Word in her womb. The promised offspring of Eve that would crush Satan's head was to be fulfilled through the birth of a Son to Mary (Genesis 3:15).

39. When Joseph was told that Mary was pregnant, he logically assumed that she had committed adultery. Even though he assumed she sinned, Joseph loved her and showed compassion. The penalty for adultery was death, yet Joseph wanted to spare Mary of this fate and planned to quietly divorce her. After the angel of the Lord appeared to Joseph and explained that Mary was to give birth to the Messiah, he submitted to the Lord and took Mary to be his wife. Joseph displays righteousness because of his love for Mary and submission to the Lord.

The Great News (Connect)

40. When reason is used over and against God's revelation of Himself, then reason separates us from God. Placing philosophical restrictions on what God can and cannot do is a sin against the First Commandment. This elevates man's natural abilities and places restrictions on God's abilities. Reason can be used in service and submission to the

Word of God. In order to understand the very sentence structures of the text of Scripture, man must use his reason. In this instance, reason aids our understanding of God.

41. Mary asked how she was able to have a child. After the angel explained it to her, she faithfully submitted. God gives us faith to humbly submit to God's Word. When the Scriptures speak, faith comprehends. When God tells us that we are sinners and deserving of death, we acknowledge in repentance. When God tells us that He has saved us from our sins by the death of His Son, we respond in praise.

42. Answers will vary. Write these ideas down and encourage the participants to take action.

For This Week

Urge the participants to pursue at least one of the suggested activities.

Closing Worship

Sing together the hymn "I Am Trusting You, Lord Jesus" (*LW* 408).